SALSA PIANO

THE COMPLETE GUIDE WITH AUDIO!

PLAYBACK+
Speed • Pitch • Balance • Loop

To access audio visit:
www.halleonard.com/mylibrary
Enter Code
3925-8206-0180-4182

BY HECTOR MARTIGNON

ISBN 978-0-634-06700-6

7777 W. BLUEMOUND RD. P.O. BOX 13819 MILWAUKEE, WI 53213

In Australia contact:
Hal Leonard Australia Pty. Ltd.
4 Lentara Court
Cheltenham, Victoria, 3192 Australia
Email: ausadmin@halleonard.com.au

Visit Hal Leonard Online at **www.halleonard.com**

INTRODUCTION

Welcome to *Salsa Piano*. If you're interested in what makes salsa music such a special genre for keyboardists, then you've come to the right place! Whatever your playing level, this book will help you play in various salsa styles, capturing all of its unique rhythmic flavor.

This book is divided in two sections: **basics** and **advanced skills**. The first one is designed to give any student, beginner or advanced, basic historical, social, and cultural background, in addition to describing the instrumental context from which the Latin piano style evolved. For example, the student will become acquainted with the percussion section of a salsa band, so as to learn how to interact with and learn from the different instruments. The harmonic structure of the examples is as simple as it gets, allowing for a stronger emphasis on the rhythmic intricacies of Latin music. After finishing this section, the student can apply all the concepts learned to any situation, in both performance and composition.

Any piano player can learn from this book. Besides possessing a relatively advanced technique, the player who studies this book should have a fundamental knowledge of music theory, and hopefully some experience in playing jazz, specifically in devising chord voicings.

Once you're finished with this book, you will be able to play and enjoy this music, both in a loose and improvisational situation, as well as in a professional setting. A gozar!!! (Enjoy!)

About the Audio

On the accompanying audio, you'll find demonstrations of most of the examples in the book, and many of the examples feature a wide variety of Latin percussion instruments, sometimes alone, but usually in combination with the piano. Please see the individual chapters for specific information on the audio tracks and how to use them. A two-measure clave pattern starts out most examples. However, these two measures are not included in the measure numbering. Measure 1 will be considered the first measure after the two-bar clave pattern. Additional musicians include **John Benitez** on bass and **Samuel Torres** on percussion.

About the Author

Hector Martignon has performed, recorded, composed, produced, and arranged music in many styles and genres for his own projects and for top musicians around the world. His solo CDs *Portrait in White and Black*, *Foreign Affair*, and *Refugee* display the diverse musical influences that have shaped his distinctive style as a performer, composer, and arranger. Since relocating to New York City, Martignon has been one of the most sought-after pianists on the Latin jazz scene. He has toured with artists such as Mongo Santamaría, Gato Barbieri, Steve Turre, and Don Byron. (Hector also recorded on Byron's latest CD.) In addition, he has been the featured pianist with the bands of Tito Puente, Mario Bauzá, Chico O'Farrill, Paquito D'Rivera, and Max Roach. Most notably, Martignon was the pianist for the late Ray Barretto's various ensembles. His collaboration with Barretto, "My Summertime," was a nominee for a GRAMMY® award.

This book is dedicated to the memory of

RAY BARRETTO

CONTENTS

Chapter 1

WHAT IS SALSA?

There are many differing, even conflicting, ideas about what salsa music is, where it comes from, and how it should be played. In the same way that people argue about sports, politics, or religion, many instrumentalists disagree on how the music in general, and their instruments in particular, should be played. I have spent years looking for an elusive "unified theory," and have come to the conclusion that there is no such thing. The foremost cause of the many discrepancies is the fact that every country or geographical region associated with salsa has developed its own style, tradition, and set of (largely unwritten) rules.

Regarding this issue, two schools of thought have evolved. One argues that salsa is mainly a product of Afro-Cuban music, and therefore the only way to understand salsa is to study Cuban music. The other contends that although salsa has Cuban roots, it developed outside of Cuba, after the revolution, mainly in New York and Puerto Rico, and later spread to many other countries that each developed their own idiosyncratic styles, independent from Cuban music.

Some of us think they are *both* right. As a matter of fact, the style that emerged in New York in the '60s, when the word "salsa" first started being used to identify a type of music, serves modern Cuban bands as a template. By the same token, bands in New York are increasingly looking to Cuba for inspiration.

The main subject of this book is how to play the piano in the style known as salsa (and, by extension, Latin jazz). But it is equally about how *not* to play. Many good jazz musicians ask for one lesson on what they call the "Latin thing." For many a good jazz musician there is no real difference between Brazilian and Afro-Cuban music. Most are not aware that there are more than a dozen rhythms the average salsa piano player has to master. Saddest of all, many have learned some generic piano pattern during their training that not only is completely at odds with tradition, but is simply tasteless.

This book will convey to the reader the way to play salsa piano that evolved specifically in New York City. Some consideration will be given to the Cuban style at those times when it constitutes a completely different alternative.

Chapter 2

A BRIEF HISTORY I
The Genesis of Caribbean Music

This chapter includes a short comparative history of salsa and the advent of the piano in the popular music of Cuba and New Orleans, as well as a comparison of piano-precursors: the banjo in the Mississippi Delta and the tres in Cuba. Early Latin pianists included Ignacio Cervantes, Noro Morales, Lino Frias, and Perez Prado.

Soon after the discovery of America and its settlement by European colonists, the Caribbean became known as the Mediterranean Sea of the New World. It was the geographical center of all commercial, political, economic, and religious activity. The exchange of goods, ideas, and people made it the first New World "melting pot." Although originally claimed exclusively by Spain, the region soon attracted the attention of other European powers (mainly France, England, and Holland) all of which launched, and with time intensified their efforts to carve out a piece of the new domains. While the continental (southern) part of the Caribbean basin, along with the major islands of Cuba and Puerto Rico, were firmly under Spanish control, most other islands were contested by several powers. Some of them passed from one to the other empire more than once, not unlike the Louisiana Territory with its capital, New Orleans.

Ships from all over the Caribbean, especially from Cuba, arrived and departed daily. The racial and cultural mix invited many travelers to stay for a while or even establish themselves in the fascinating city of New Orleans. Among those travelers were many Cubans or Spaniards that had left Cuba after the Spanish-American War.

One of the results of such a convergence of nations and peoples was the emergence of one of the most prolific cultural "laboratories" in history. This lab brought forth a fountain of artistic expression and revolutionary political ideas.

There are many factors that have led anthropologists, historians, and ethnomusicologists to the conclusion that the city of New Orleans is in many ways a Caribbean city. Looking at its cultural roots, geographic position, religious expressions, Carnival, and last but not least, its music with the ubiquitous marching bands, you can easily find commonalities with such cities as San Juan, Cartagena, Port au Prince, Veracruz, and any major city in the Caribbean rim, most of all Havana.

What the blues meant to the history of jazz in the southern United States is in many ways similar to the importance of the **son montuno** in the development of Afro-Cuban music. Both have eminently rural origins; both are vehicles for transmitting renditions of local events mostly associated with agricultural chores, grievances, and love stories; and both rely on the guitar (or a derivative thereof) to provide the main harmonic and melodic structure.

On the other hand, during the swing era many bands from Cuba were invited to share stages with the great swing big bands. The rumba craze started in April of 1936, with Don Aspiazu's Havana Casino Orchestra performing at New York's Palace Theater. The '40s brought a greater sophistication in orchestration, with many bands acquiring a taste for big-band-jazz arrangements, and in the process adding what can be defined as final cultural influence in Cuban music.

A crucial juncture in the history of Afro-Cuban music came along with the Cuban revolution in early 1959. Commercial relations between Cuba and the U.S.A. quickly broke down. The exchange of goods, people, and ideas was thwarted by the embargo imposed on the island, with one of the consequences being that copyrights and intellectual property were no longer recognized. Savvy businesspeople and music executives started producing music based on Cuban rhythms and songs, marketing the trend as a purely indigenous

New York cultural phenomenon. Many Cuban hits were recorded without acknowledging the composers or the bands that had originally recorded the songs. Eventually most traces of the music's Cuban origins disappeared into oblivion, while at the same time a truly authentic New York sound started to emerge. This opened the doors to input from other, non-Cuban, sources, i.e., musicians from other Latin American countries, American jazz musicians, and most of all, the already established musicians from Puerto Rico.

After the strictly Cuban rumba and mambo crazes of the '40s and '50s, a new cultural phenomenon appeared in the '60s, together with a stronger sense of pride and national belonging on the part of the Puerto Rican population of New York City. Not surprisingly, their music contained new nuances that gave it a very particular flavor, like pouring a new *sauce* on top of a familiar dish: **salsa**.

No one knows exactly when and where the word "salsa" was first used to describe a type of music, or who, for that matter, came up with the idea. Cuban music was already part of the popular imagination in the New Orleans of the early twentieth century, not only through cultural elements inherited from the Spanish colonization of Louisiana, but through the vast exchange of ideas and goods taking place through the port of the city.

Meanwhile, the United States' cultural influence in Cuba swiftly replaced Spain's after the Spanish-American War. Among the results of these developments was the arrival in the great Cuban hotels of some of the best jazz big bands, which didn't pass unnoticed to the local musicians and arrangers.

What most people can safely agree upon is that the origins of many salsa rhythms lie in Cuba and the many cultures that merged on, and emerged from, that Caribbean island.

Chapter 3
A BRIEF HISTORY II
Cuban Music, The Piano, and Early Players

There were three main streams of cultural tradition flowing into each other in Cuban music toward the beginning of the twentieth century: son montuno, rumba, and danzón.

The rural, mostly Spanish-influenced **son montuno** (literally, "mountain sound") was played by the peasants on Spanish guitar, bongos from northern Africa (by way of Spain), maracas (one of a few Native American contributions to Cuban music), and a type of guitar imported by immigrants from the Canary Islands that featured three double strings, fittingly called the **tres**. A strong flamenco reminiscence can be heard in early recordings of this music, particularly those by Celina y Reutilio and the Trio Matamoros.

The African, mainly Yoruba, culture was inherited by the descendants of slaves. Because few of them owned farmland, this culture was mainly urban. Their music, featuring mostly percussion and a kind of "call and response" singing, can be grouped under the somewhat arbitrary name of **rumba**, given the dominance of this rhythm in all its structures. (This rumba has of course nothing to do with the ballroom rhumba later marketed in the U.S.)

The third addition to this confluence of cultures came from the French **contredanse** (which itself derived from the English **country dance**). During the French exodus from Haiti in the early nineteenth century, at least some of the people moved across the windward passage into the eastern part of Cuba, called **Oriente**. Already a hotbed of many musical styles, Oriente rivaled Havana and the western provinces in cultural output. Matanzas, Santiago, and the Camagüey province had their own styles based upon the son montuno. The French brought with them a strong tradition of chamber music, which included the popular dances of nineteenth-century France, foremost the contredanse. Out of this developed the **danzón**, which became Cuba's national dance. On January 1, 1879, at a school ball in Matanzas, the orchestra of Miguel Failde performed the first danzón ever heard in Cuba. The style developed in Cuba by these groups received the name of **charanga francesa**, and later simply **charanga**. The instrumentation of the charanga ensembles included a string section, one or two flutes, and a set of orchestral timpani.

The guitar (and myriad other instruments derived from it) was the central instrument of most musical activity in Spain's American colonies. Guitar-like instruments included the **tres** in Cuba, the Puerto Rican **cuatro** (not to be confused with the typical **cuatro** found in the Venezuelan and Colombian central plains), and the **tiple** from Colombia (actually derived from the **triple** from the Canary Islands). All these instruments were central to the vernacular musical expressions of their respective countries.

In Cuba the most prevalent stringed instrument was the tres. This is basically a modified guitar with six strings, arranged in three double courses, each pair of strings tuned in octaves to the notes G-G, C-C, and E-E to give the sound of a C major chord. The decision to apply the six strings of the guitar to three double courses was likely made to give it more volume in the presence of percussion instruments, thereby sacrificing voices for enhanced audibility. As a direct consequence of this rearrangement of the strings of the guitar, the instrument is mostly played one note at a time, chords being outlined as arpeggios rather than with a full strum. This is pivotal to our understanding of the piano in a salsa context, given the fact that it was intended to imitate (and often even to double) its predecessor the tres. The tres was the main instrument of the Cuban son band. Around 1920, the **sexteto** format became popular, featuring a tres, guitar, string bass, bongos, and two singers doubling on claves and maracas. In the late '20s, groups began to add a trumpet, transforming the sexteto into the **septeto**. It was Arsenio Rodriguez, arguably the greatest of all tres players on record, who in the 1940s expanded the folkloric sextetos and septetos, adding piano, conga, and multiple trumpets, creating something he called **conjunto tipico**. It is the first time that the piano (and for that matter, the conga) finds a voice in a popular Cuban dance band. The piano player limited himself mostly to doubling the figures performed by the tres player.

As mentioned earlier, playing full chords on the tres is not very easy, and are thus usually arpeggiated as single notes or played, at most, two notes at a time. This gives us two clues as to how to outline a harmonic sequence at the piano in an authentic Afro-Cuban manner: play in octaves or fifteenths, thereby imitating the double courses of the tres; and play the chords as arpeggios instead of striking each chord all at once (as one would do in jazz).

The following is an example of a typical piano figure imitating a tres player. We will analyze this example in Chapter 6, but for now, just take a quick look and listen to familiarize yourself.

As with many of the audio tracks, slight variation may occur on repeats, as a real salsa band would rarely play the exact same thing twice.

Typical piano figure

Although the piano substituted for the tres in most orchestras, today many prestigious bands in New York and Puerto Rico feature a tres player along with the piano, and the playing of the two is highly coordinated

TRACK 1

and effective. This is not the case in Cuba, where hardly any modern band uses the tres. Only a typical son montuno band would use the traditional instrument instead of the piano, not only for the sake of authenticity, but also for the simple reason that those groups are frequently on the move from one tavern to the next.

Chapter 4

THE RHYTHM SECTION

No matter how much a pianist knows about salsa, it won't be of any help if he or she doesn't understand the rhythmic context within which the piano plays, how it interacts as part of a perfectly coordinated rhythm box, the result of decades (if not centuries) of evolution.

All music played in a salsa band follows an underlying, uniting principle that governs everything in the way people sing, play, and dance. It is a legacy from mother Africa that arrived centuries ago in the Americas and can be identified in the streets of New Orleans, Havana, Barranquilla, San Juan, Rio de Janeiro, and all the way to Montevideo.

Clave

This rhythmic foundation is called **clave**, often translated into English as "code" or "key." The instruments most likely to play this pattern are two: the timbales and the aptly named claves, two approximately eight-inch long sticks of heavy wood played against each other. The real origin of this instrument seems to be the "clavos" or nails used to secure the sails of the slave ships crossing the Atlantic. Slaves on those ships were prompted to play and dance during the long journey, not as a means of entertainment, but in order to keep them physically fit. Often the only instruments available on board were those large wooden nails, from which the slaves got the sound and the rhythms nowadays associated with claves. The word "clave," then, refers not only to the instrument (the pair of claves often included in the Latin percussion section), but also—and more crucially for our purposes—to a rhythmic pattern at the heart of salsa music.

As we will see later, there are countless types of clave patterns, but one stands out as something of a rallying cry with which fans and musicians alike associate salsa. We will call it **son clave**:

Son clave

TRACK 2

Play 5 times

It has been the subject of countless dissertations, discussion panels, late-night conversations, and not infrequently (to which I can attest) the cause of fistfights. Some people even insist vehemently that *all* music has some kind of clave, and if you have an open mind and a little imagination you will start to agree with this statement and hear clave all over the place. More than just a specific pattern, it can be considered a framing concept for many types of rhythms.

One of the most common claves identifiable in many parts of sub-Saharan Africa is the following 6/8 pattern:

6/8 clave

TRACK 3

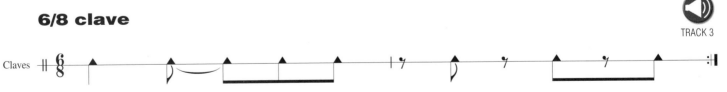

This pattern is ubiquitous not only in western and southern Africa, but throughout the Caribbean and Brazil as well. Many scholars consider this to be the mother of all Afro-Caribbean claves, especially those used in the music called rumba (not to be confused with ballroom rhumba!).

Taking the first, second, fourth, fifth, and sixth hits of the previous clave and phrasing it in a 4/4 meter results in the **rumba clave**.

Rumba clave

In fact, there are variations of rumba that use the 6/8 clave while two of the three drums (the low-pitched **tumbadora**) play a 6/8 pattern as well. This is all done while the mid-range tres and high-pitched **quinto** improvise in 4/4! Moreover, when a percussionist in a salsa band is asked to play an "Afro," he immediately starts playing the 6/8 clave.

It is revealing to compare these two claves. Listen to the audio, on which the two claves are played at the same time:

6/8 and rumba clave at the same time

As we progress, we will learn how the different kinds of clave dictate how to play the piano. But first we will continue with the rest of the rhythm section.

The percussion section

The typical salsa percussion section has three large instruments: **congas**, **timbales**, and **bongos**; and several smaller hand instruments like **maracas**, **guiro**, and an extra set of claves. One must first become familiar with the backbone of the section, the most "African" of the three large instruments: the congas. Most likely originally from areas populated by the Congo people, the congas are two barrel-shaped instruments with an animal skin strung across the upper opening, their pitch being determined by their size as well as by the tension applied to the skin. Most people tune them to G1 and C1, with a possible third one at D1. The next example shows the most common pattern played by two congas; with some variation on the repeats:

Conga pattern

Now is a good time to acquaint yourself with the role of the clave: note that only two notes are played on the low conga (tumbadora). The note played in the first bar corresponds exactly to the second (♩) note of the son clave (on the "and" of 2), while the one in the second bar likewise corresponds to the clave's ♩ (second hit of the second bar). Understanding this is of vital importance, since it illustrates the subordination of all the instruments to the structure given by the clave pattern. We will soon show how this applies to the salsa piano player.

The **timbales** are instruments derived from the classical timpani, which arrived in eastern Cuba in the nineteenth century, when the French fled Haiti following its independence. Moving to eastern Cuba, the French brought with them the typical chamber music ensemble they used in their social events, featuring a small string section, a peculiar E♭ soprano flute called the **tercerolle**, and a small percussion section that included a pair of symphonic timpani.

In the Oriente region of eastern Cuba, the most beautiful music evolved from the interweaving of French and native musical cultures. The French "contredanse" became "contradanza" and "danzón" from which later, in the twentieth century, emerged the "charanga" style. The percussion section of the **danzón** can be heard on audio track 13.

Eventually the timpani became smaller, home-made instruments, played with straight, small drumsticks instead of mallets. These are the timbales we now see in every salsa band. Their role is similar to that of the drums in the jazz big band: not only keeping time, but also accentuating all the important hits played by the horns, and preparing all orchestral breaks. The following illustrates a typical timbales figure:

Typical timbales figure

TRACK 7

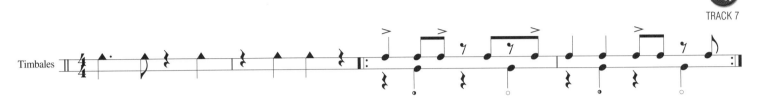

The right hand plays the bell on top of the timbales while the left hand plays, open handed, on beat 2 with a "slap" and on beat 4, an open sound, in both bars. This figure and its particular sound, reminiscent of the timpani playing danzón, has been termed **sobao** ("rubbed").

The third main large instrument is the pair of bongos. They are similar to the congas, but much smaller and higher-pitched. The performer improvises through much of the theme in the main section of a tune, then abandons the bongos in favor of a big cow bell or campana in the montuno (a repetitious part of the tune, or vamp, where most of the instrumental and vocal improvisation takes place). The musician then retakes the bongos to finish the tune.

The following is a likely pattern around which the bongo player would improvise. It is known as **martillo** ("hammer").

Martillo

TRACK 8

The **bongocero** is the only instrumentalist in a salsa band to play more than one instrument in almost every tune, playing alternately the bongos and the **cowbell** (or **campana**). The cowbell brings a strong new color to the percussion section and invites the dancers to become more creative in their figures, including the possibility of dancing separately at some moments. It also indicates to the piano player that he should switch to a more repetitive pattern, one reminiscent of the original music after which this section is named: **montuno**, as in son montuno.

Cowbell pattern I

Below is one possible cowbell pattern; the lower line indicates to play the open sound on the bell, performed at the edge of the instrument:

TRACK 9

We will go into more depth regarding the cowbell in the following chapters because of its close relationship and coordination with the piano.

The Bass

The **bass** is the instrument that not only provides the harmonic foundation to the whole, but also—along with the conga—keeps the band together rhythmically. Its harmonic root is played mostly on the fourth beat, while the fifth and other bass notes are played on the "and" of 2 or on 3 which, as we will eventually learn, depends on which clave is been played. If there is something distinctive and immediately recognizable in salsa, it is that the bass hardly ever plays on beat 1 of the bar. That makes the music seem so foreign and exotic to untrained listeners, and difficult to grasp both as a player and as a dancer.

Let's look at a **tumbao**, a typical bass pattern, noting the similarity with the clave pattern displayed above it. Also note that, after the first time through, the bass part undergoes some slight variation (as would happen in a real musical situation):

Tumbao

TRACK 10

Now the reader may wonder why it is that we have to write the clave, and with it *all* the music, in two separate bars instead of in just one bar like the following:

Clave notated in one bar

The answer to this question is at the core of this book—understanding this is pivotal in learning how to play piano, or any instrument for that matter, in a salsa context. It is important to be able to split the clave pattern in two. This makes it possible to invert the pattern, reversing the order of the two bars. That way, instead of the following example…

3-2 clave

…the whole structure of the music can revolve around the pattern shown below…

2-3 clave

TRACK 11

…or its rumba variant.

Rumba clave

TRACK 12

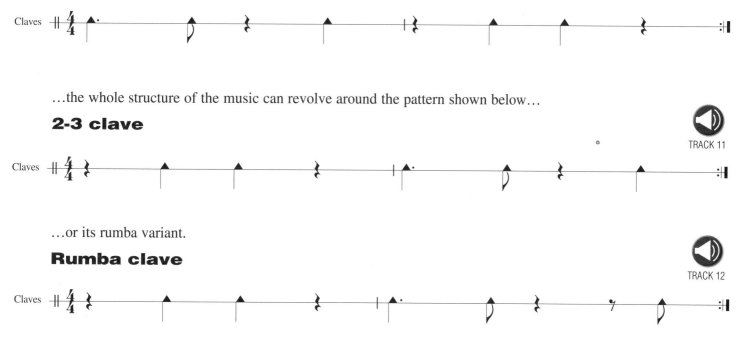

Since in the first pattern the first bar has three notes and the second bar two, this clave has been named *3-2 clave*. It follows that when the pattern is inverted—two notes in the first and three notes in the second bar—it is referred to as *2-3 clave*.

Most of the tunes in salsa start with a 3-2 clave structure. Then, when the middle section (called montuno) occurs, the whole band shifts to a sort of "second gear." This is the section where the singer and instrumentalists will improvise within a two-, four-, or eight-measure vamp; it usually uses a 2-3 clave structure, which seems to be better for dancing. In order to get from 3-2 to 2-3 clave, the composer or the arranger slips in an orchestral break of an uneven number of bars—three, five, or even 7. Because of the uneven number of bars, after the break is over the clave will be in the second bar of its pattern (the 2 part), effectively turning upside-down. Now the pattern will be 2-3. After a second, similar break, the tune turns around again to its original 3-2 structure, often retaking the introduction or the bridge of the song as a reprise.

The clave pattern can be described as a succession of five hits, labelled in this book with circled numerals: ①, ②, ③, ④, ⑤. This is true for *clave de son* or *clave de rumba*, whether the pattern is 3-2 or 2-3. For example:

3-2 clave

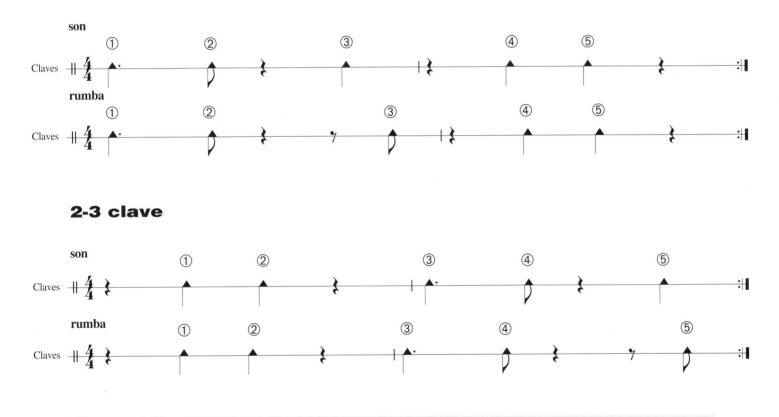

We will refer to the bar with three hits as the "3" bar of the clave, and the bar with two hits as the "2" bar of the clave.

As we move along, we will penetrate further into this fascinating realm. At the beginning of Chapter 5, you will find a good description of a full percussion section in a 2-3 clave environment. For now, having learned a little bit about the history, function, and rhythmic structure of the typical salsa rhythm section, we are ready to study the way the piano fits into the family, as a harmonic, percussive, and sometimes melodic instrument.

Chapter 5
3-2 CLAVE PATTERNS IN SINGLE-HARMONY DESCARGA

This chapter holds a special place in the progress of this book. We will analyze fundamental rhythmic patterns that apply to most sections in 3-2 clave, independently of how harmonically complex they might be. Internalizing the material in this chapter is crucial to understanding the rest of the book.

TRACK 13

Take a quick listen to audio track 13 to get a historical perspective on the structure of the 3-2 clave. You'll hear a rhythm-section part of the venerable danzón, a French-influenced rhythm derived from the contredanse, which arrived in Cuba toward the middle of the nineteenth century.

Now let's look at the most basic of all progressions, one that is used in a myriad of situations as a framework to jam and improvise to for hours on end, the **descarga**, meaning "discharge." Harmonically, it consists of only one chord—a dominant seventh chord, alternating with a suspended version of itself.

Since for some reason it is played mostly in C7, this progression has earned its own humorous generic name: "Si se ven," roughly translated into English as "if they see each other" but pronounced "C seven" (C7). Some bandleaders might even call a tune, screaming "let's play *Si se ven* in F!"—meaning, of course, F7.

Though it may seem like an odd pedagocial tactic, we will start with the typical figure a non-Latin player would play, which in some ways is considered to be wrong:

Typical non-Latin figure

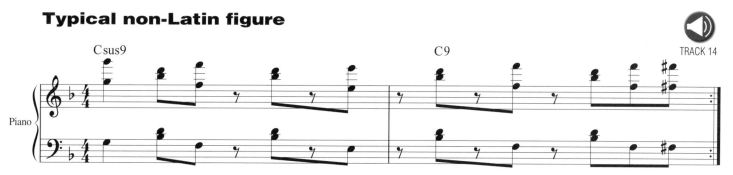

TRACK 14

> *The clearest and most obvious way a pianist outlines the clave structure is with octaves in the right hand. The left hand exactly doubles it rhythmically, and MOSTLY, but not always, melodically. This style clearly echoes (as described in Chapter 1) the patterns played by tres players in the son montuno bands that preceded the modern salsa orchestras.*

The previous example is a decent method for "getting out of the way": a pattern providing a solid harmonic frame that is universally used when a clear clave structure is not recognizable (which, by the way, is very often the case). Rhythmically, this piano part lacks a clear accentuation of the third beat of the second bar (which would be the second strike of the clave in the "2" part of 3-2), making it ambiguous whether or not the pianist knows what clave is being played. In this sense it is fool-proof.

Some people would argue that this is definitely a pattern obeying a 3-2 clave because the first bar plays strongly on beat 1 as in the clave pattern. This rule has been used as a general guide in this difficult matter, but it is only partially true and an extremely limiting option. We'll discuss this more as we advance.

Depending upon what the bass line does, the following progression could be interpreted harmonically in two ways: as a Gm7–C9 sequence, or a Csus9–C9 sequence.

Gm7–C9 sequence

Csus9–C9 sequence:

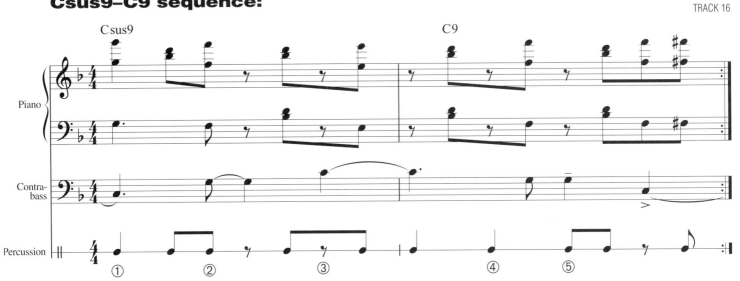

As described in Chapter 4, one way of creating interesting montunos is to follow the patterns played by the bongocero with his cowbell. In a 3-2 environment this would be a typical (if somewhat boring) pattern:

Cowbell pattern I

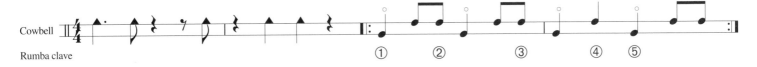

There is not much a pianist can learn from the information provided by this pattern. Not until the bongocero starts adding variations does it become interesting. One such variation is shown in the following example:

Cowbell pattern II—bongocero variation

Comparing this with the next example, you will see many hits coinciding. Watch out for variations on the audio with each repeat.

This is one of the most common ways of playing a 3-2 pattern with conviction in a strictly salsa dance band. Comparing the previous two examples, you will see that the only big difference is that the cowbell is playing the first beat in *both* the first and the second bars, while the piano binds the last eighth note of the second bar with the first eighth note of the first bar. This is a beautifully structured 3-2 pattern that combines two different tendencies, accentuating some and circumventing other beats of the clave.

Now we arrive at a difficult juncture: it is widely accepted that pianists in Cuba tend to play *around* the clave, skillfully and artfully filling its gaps, while consciously avoiding accentuating the beats. However, their counterparts in New York City (and other places influenced by New York City) will try to accentuate as many of the beats of the clave as possible. Analyzing the "Typical non-Latin piano figure" from the beginning of this chapter, we notice that the first and second beats of the "3" part of the 3-2 are accentuated by the piano while the two beats in the "2" part are avoided.

In our most recent example, we can see how beats ②, ④, and ⑤ of the 3-2 clave are being affirmed by the pianist, while ① and ③ have been circumvented. Still, this is the way most pianists in New York City would play the 3-2 clave.

Let's look at another, even more interesting, cowbell figure:

Cowbell pattern III

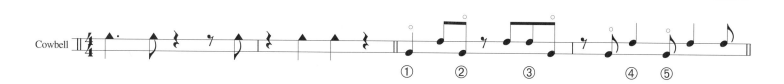

> *Many Cuban musicians argue that there is no distinction between 3-2 and 2-3 clave, but rather that there is only one pattern that is sometimes turned around by uneven numbers of bars in different sections. In fact, most tunes in Cuba start in 3-2 and in the montuno section turn into 2-3, as described at the end of Chapter 4. The musicians would say the clave NEVER changed.*

2-3 CLAVE PATTERNS IN SINGLE-HARMONY DESCARGA

Most of the principles that apply to the way the pianist builds his playing in a 3-2 clave setting apply also to the 2-3. At first sight, that is easily achieved simply by reversing the order of the two bars that make up the clave, including only the rhythmical elements, while the harmonic sequences are dealt with in an independent manner.

Let's look at the structure of the percussion in a 2-3 environment.

Percussion in a 2-3 environment

TRACK 20

First of all, notice that the clave being used here accentuates (at hit ☐) the "and" of the fourth beat of the second bar (the "3" bar). What does this tell us? It means we will be using the rumba clave, also (inappropriately) called **clave Cubana**. Players choose this clave because, especially in a medium to fast tempo, it is a more even way of spacing the hits in the two bars of the clave. Also note in the following example that the figure played by the timbales accentuates the "and" of the second bar's fourth beat as well. This has no bearing on the way the claves player structures his/her pattern.

Timbales figure

TRACK 21

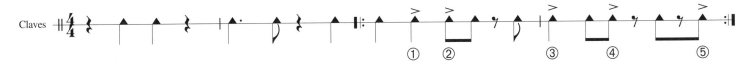

This, by the way, is no trivial matter. There are dozens of rhythms in salsa. Some examples (ordered from slow to fast) include bolero, guajira, cha-cha, guaracha, and guaguanccó. As explained in Chapter 3, these rhythms, as well as countless others, evolved from two main sources: the son montuno and the rumba. The first has a stronger Spanish influence, while the latter's origins point unmistakably to the African traditions imported mostly from Nigeria's Yoruba culture and the Congolese from southern West Africa. While the son montuno relies more strongly on a 4/4 subdivision, the rumba sounds clearly like a 2/2 (alla breve) time signature. This dictates a different way of feeling the clave.

Son clave

TRACK 11

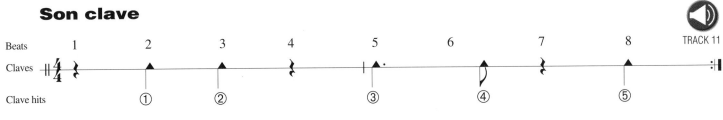

The son clave underlies a subdivision of eight beats (four per bar), while the rumba clave, in many ways more sophisticated and flexible, obeys a subdivision of four beats (two per bar).

Rumba clave

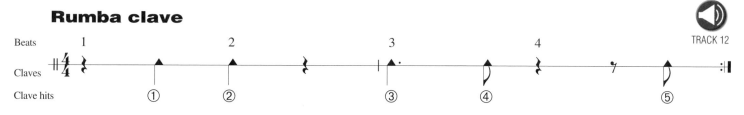

The differences between son and rumba can also cause discrepancies in the way the piano is played. It all boils down to the ⑤ hit of the clave in 2-3 or the ③ hit in 3-2.

Piano with son clave

TRACK 22

Notice that measures 5–8 are the resolution of the C7 chord implied in measures 1–4. In Chapter 7 the whole II-V-I sequence will be discussed.

This is an archetypical **tumbao** based on the venerable Cuban tres. Note that the only difference in the piano part between the "2" bar and the "3" bar of the clave pattern is the last note of each bar: in the first bar the last note falls on the "and" of the fourth beat, but in the second bar, the same note falls right on the fourth beat, the ▯ hit of the clave.

It would be advisable to check out original recordings of the greatest tres players, most notably Arsenio Rodriguez, to get a feeling of where the piano playing comes from. As discussed in Chapter 3, he is the one who introduced the piano into Cuban ensembles, at that time called septetos típicos.

Note that both hands play exactly the same notes two octaves apart. Although the individual courses of the tres are tuned only one octave apart, on the piano many salsa musicians prefer the sound and color achieved when the interval between the notes is two octaves. Also note that in the seventh and ninth bars, the bass plays the third beat of the "2" bar—the ② hit of the 2-3 clave. This is by no means a strict rule, but most bass players do play this beat every once in a while just to cement the "2" bar of the clave while at the same time guiding the dancers, who would have to decide whether to start on the "2" in the case of 2-3, or on the "1" in 3-2.

> *It is important to consider the possibility that no claves player will be around to guide your playing. This is often the case—either for economic reasons, or more often than not, by design. It is generally assumed that all players know their roles and the particular way their instruments imply or reinforce the clave structure. In other words, clave is implicit and not explicit.*

We already mentioned the way the bass player sometimes implies the "2" side of the clave by accentuating the ② hit. Moreover, the bassist will try to play the lowest possible note on the fourth beat of the "3" bar in a 2-3 environment, accentuating the ⑤ hit.

Below we have the clearest possible way to outline the 2-3 clave:

Outlining the clave: tumbao

TRACK 23

This **tumbao** obeys the already mentioned principle that recommends always playing the first beat of the "2" bar. Remember, if you obey this principle, you will always be right; but if you don't, you won't necessarily be wrong. It also clearly accentuates the ①, the ②, and the ④ hits of the clave. In New York City, you will be greatly appreciated for providing a very clear structure, both for the instrumentalists and the dancers. Still, if you always play this way, the band is going to sound somewhat square and monotonous. You will soon be looking for more options to make your montunos interesting and lively.

In certain situations, the pianist can become somewhat "busier," playing the chords as arpeggios, imitating the idiosyncratic playing of the tres.

Piano imitation of the tres

TRACK 24

The descending line (G–F–E) outlined by the octaves in the right hand, and doubled by the left hand two octaves lower, gives us the ② and the ④ hits of the 2-3 clave. These are the most important hits of this clave (as would be hits ② and ⑤ in 3-2). These are the most important hits of this clave (as would be hits ② and ⑤ in 3-2). In both cases these hits frame the rhythmic structure, alternating between the third beat of one bar (hit ② in 2-3 and hit ⑤ in 3-2) and the "and" of the second beat of the other bar (hit ④ in 2-3 and hit ② in 3-2).

> *Arpeggiating the chords (in other words, spreading the notes of the chord over the available eighths) can be very useful in at least two situations: at slow tempos (as we will see in the case of the Guajiras) or in very intense sections, where the piano is asked to keep playing while the rest of the band lays off—a devise typically used by Cuban bands to raise the level of intensity, and prolong the tune.*

For now, this basic information should suffice for you to start creating your own tumbaos. You may do so in one of two fashions: by imitating the tres style; or by outlining the clave with the first beat of the "2" bar, and at least the ② hit of the clave (the third beat of the same bar).

We will see how further variations can be developed by shifting the main accents, either by repeating certain portions of the pattern or by delaying the resolution of the pattern into one of the main hits of the clave. In this endeavor, the octaves of the right hand play an especially important role by defining the accents.

Once you have understood the principles and concepts outlined in Chapters 5 and 6, you can embark on rhythmically, harmonically, and melodically more intricate and adventurous tumbaos.

Chapter 7

MONTUNOS FOR MAJOR AND MINOR II–V–I

Having understood the basics of 2-3 and 3-2 clave as applied to a simple harmonic sequence, we can proceed to expand the harmonic frame. The obvious first step is the II–V–I progression, a very familiar one in the world of jazz, Caribbean music and, for that matter, most music of the world. The first example is in 2-3 clave and shows a series of variations on that progression, with one bar each for the II and V harmonies and two bars for the tonic or I chord. It is played almost in unison, using both hands, with only slight differences from repetition to repetition. The following are the first two cycles of four bars each.

Montuno #1

TRACK 25

Note that with F as the tonic in this example, II is Gm7 and V (the dominant) is C7. This makes it possible to use the knowledge acquired in the two preceding chapters and apply it to the expanded progression, one that features the resolution of that original Gm7 (II) and C7 (V) into Fmaj (I).

The main difference between the two cycles is that in **1)** the right hand doubles at the octave all notes played with the thumb, accentuating the main rhythmical positions of the clave, while in **2)** sometimes one hand arpeggiates what the other is playing as a chord (as in measure 5), or the hands play in opposite directions (as in measure 7).

Other differences among the consecutive II-V-I cycles are more subtle and relevant. For example, look at the beginning of the second cycle: the first beat is a rest for both hands. The root of the chord has been anticipated in the preceding bar, which makes it unnecessary to play it again on the downbeat (this also happens in the third bar of each four-bar cycle)—providing that it is not really obligatory to play the down-beat in the "2" part of the clave. In fact, the only strong beat throughout this example is the ② hit of the clave (the third beats of the first, third, fifth, and seventh bars).

The next example uses an identical harmonic pattern, but each hand complements the other harmonically, thus enriching the color with a more dissonant, "jazzy" sound, one that became very popular in New York City by the late '80s. The example also shows how it is not uncommon to emphasize the clave strongly, mostly at the beginning, only to give way later to arpeggios in subsequent cycles.

Montuno #2

TRACK 26

At the downbeat of the first bar, the left hand starts with an F, the seventh of the Gm7 chord, while the right hand plays the ninth, A. Two other chord tones (B♭ and D) are played on beat 2. In the next bar, the seventh (the F in the left hand from the "and" of beat 4 in bar 1) resolves to E (on the "and" of 2 in bar 2), which is the third of the dominant, C7. In the right hand, the ninth moves chromatically down to A♭, the flat thirteenth of C7. In the left hand, the last eighth of the second bar anticipates the next chord, in this case the tonic Fmaj7, giving us the strongly dissonant major seventh, with the major ninth in the right hand. In the third bar, the downbeat has been avoided. Here, an eighth note on the "and" of beat 1 precedes the clear ① and ② hits of the clave. In bars 5–8, a II–V–I is inserted to revert to Gminor7 in measure 9. Note the 9th of Aminor7, a very dissonant B natural moving down through B♭ to A, the 9th of Gminor7. This kind of dissonance can happen often enough and should be used with utmost care, specifically by letting it ring only briefly.

Another common situation arises when the rhythm section is playing at its most intense, and the pianist needs to add another notch to that collective "trance." The most obvious way to do this is by making the piano stress its percussive nature, looking for one note to be repeated constantly. This note should be one that is common to all chords in the sequence. In major tonalities, the sixth of the tonic chord is a very good candidate to contribute to this welcomed monotony. Besides being the sixth of the I chord, it is also the fifth of II, the eleventh of III, the third of IV, and the ninth of V.

The next example shows a way to use this trick, one that permits the piano to become a more integrated part not only of the rhythm section, but also of the percussion section.

Percussive piano: repeating the sixth scale degree

TRACK 27

This example brings us back to a more traditional interpretation of our sequence, one that relies heavily on the percussive character of the piano. Here we have an arpeggio whose center of gravity is the sixth of the tonic (in this case D, marked by **X**), which is played six times. In the II chord, Gm7, it is the fifth; and in the dominant, C7, it is the ninth, making it in effect a C9. In many ways, this reminds us of those fantastic riffs improvised by saxophone sections of the big band era, particularly in songs using the blues form backing up a swinging solo. In fact, this almost obsessive repetitiousness is often used behind percussion solos.

As in Brazilian music, traditional Afro-Cuban guitar playing has the tendency to avoid big jumps in the position of the hand, thereby keeping the notes as close as possible from one chord to the next. This, on top of the need to accentuate the percussive nature of the music, has led to the kind of pattern described above, where one specific note keeps being repeated almost obsessively. Oddly enough, what gives this music, and many others like it, its energy and drive is this kind of trance-like monotony, a repetitiousness that, paraphrasing Dizzy Gillespie, makes "swing" possible.

Minor keys

There are no major differences when it comes to II–V–I in minor keys, except for a slightly different harmonic rhythm. After the tonic, the possibility exists of adding an extra IV chord, instead of staying on the tonic for two bars or adding a turnaround to go back to the II. If not the arranger, it is the bass player who could decide to stay in F minor in the fourth bar of this next example. In such a case, the D of the third bar simply becomes the thirteenth (add6) of F minor instead of the third of B♭7.

Minor II–V–I

TRACK 28

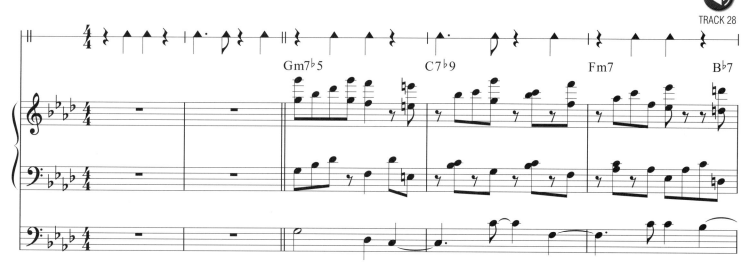

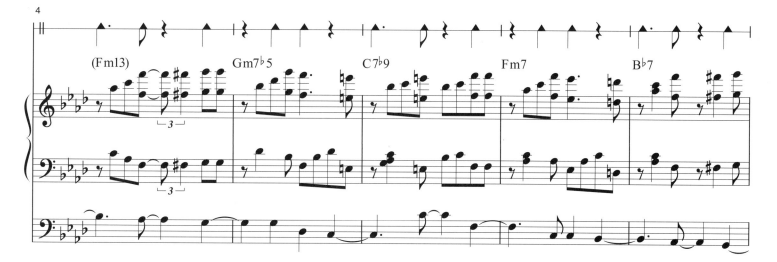

In this example, we delve into some of the most sophisticated rhythmic variations encountered in this book. Some of the intricacies depicted here are not easily notated with conventional means! We could describe some of it as an expression of personal and regional idiosyncrasies. At some point, it just simply depends on the amount of "swing" the player would be willing to involve in his performance and how much of it will be appropriate to the environment. In New York City dance bands, for example, the use of such rhythmic experimentation is (understandably) not greatly appreciated. Most singers, dancers, and even some percussionists could get confused and request a simpler and more "solid" performance from you. Still, in Latin jazz and in some progressive dance bands, this kind of playing could find an excellent reception!

Now let's see how we can open the chords harmonically to create a more complex and dissonant sound, making the right hand play a 10th (in some instances we should add an octave) above the left hand. Further variations in this example retain the harmonic and melodic structure of the pattern. The rhythmic structure is what is slightly modified each time, without changing the basic principle underlying it all—the 2-3 clave, etc.

Minor II–V–I variation

TRACK 29

Most interesting in this F minor example is the treatment given to the seventh (E♭) of the tonic. This tells us that in minor mode, things are not as straightforward as in major mode. From the beginning, the seventh (F) of the II chord does indeed resolve to the 3rd (E♮) of the V chord on the "and" of 4 in the first measure. This then resolves to the seventh (E♭) of the I chord by the "and" of 4 in the second measure.

In minor tonalities, we can also apply the principle of common-note repetition. Given that the sixth of the tonic doesn't work in the II chord (which normally has to be half diminished), the best candidate seems to be the eleventh of the I chord. In F minor, this means B♭, which is the third of the II chord and the seventh of the V chord. This works perfectly well, but only if the left hand plays the regular seventh to third, third to seventh sequence while the right hand keeps the B♭ as the percussive tone (i.e., the seventh of the II chord, F, resolves to the third of the V7 chord, E. B♭ is a common note between both chords). Basically you are playing two different montunos at the same time. The following example will demonstrate:

Repetition of the 11th (B♭)

TRACK 30

In this and similar variations where both hands play different notes, the pianist's playing diverges considerably from the original "template" given to us by the venerable masters of the tres. For example, instead of both hands playing more or less exactly the same notes in octaves, it can take advantage of the obvious possibility of playing two different parts of the chord, adding to the harmonic and melodic richness of the sound. This shows how the piano, while incrementally replacing the tres in most Latin dance bands, slowly conquered its own space in the rhythm section and developed a musical language particular to its vast possibilities.

Extended II–V–I

This section shows how to deal with the same harmonic sequence, but within an eight-bar unit. The first example prolongs a traditional tres pattern by simply repeating the original figure.

8-bar sequence

TRACK 31

Now let's apply the pattern in which the seventh of the II chord resolves to the third of the V chord, which then becomes the seventh of the I chord.

II–V–I eight-bar sequence

TRACK 32

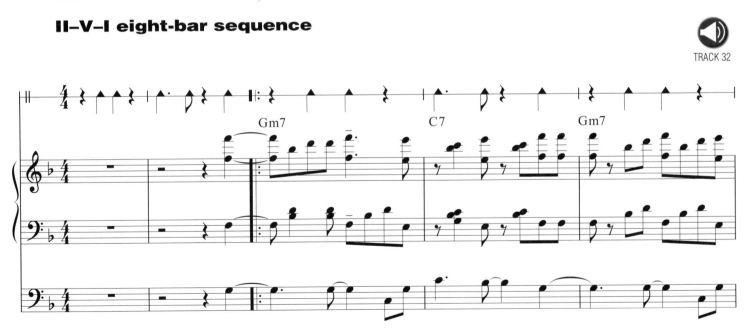

If the situation is such that the pianist and the bass player have their own discretion to interpret the instructions given by the arranger, they can decide among themselves how to treat the prolonged II-V section of the first four bars. There are many options: bar 1, II; bar 2, V; bar 3, II; bar 4, V; bar 5, I. Another option would be bar 1, II; bar 2, II; bar 3, II; bar 4, II–V; bar 5, I. Yet another option would make a good use of our original C7 material: bar 1, V; bar 2, V; bar 3, V; bar 4, II–V; bar 5, I. For the piano, not much changes from one version to the other except that the seventh to third resolution could be delayed until the end of the fourth bar before the resolution into the tonic (the B-flats resolving to A's).

Let's now add, in the right hand, a parallel voice a 10th apart. This is similar to what we did in the "Minor II–V–I" example in this chapter.

Parallel 10ths

TRACK 33

* Some variations are present on repeat.

Pay special attention to the II–VI–II turnaround in the last bar. As in Montuno #2, the right hand plays a B♮, a 10th apart from the G played by the left hand, thereby adding a strong and interesting, albeit short-lived, dissonance above the bass A.

Behind a percussion solo, we can again resort to the very idiosyncratic language of the tres, outlining the harmonies in unison.

Please note the slightly different notation used here; ♪ 𝅘𝅥 ♪ 𝅘𝅥 ♪ is written instead of ♪ 𝅘𝅥 𝅘𝅥 to accentuate the percussive nature of this pattern.

Tres-like II–V–I

TRACK 34

We can now apply these ideas to the minor mode. Using the principle of the seventh of one chord resolving to the third of the next chord (like in the "II–V–I Eight-bar sequence" example in this chapter), we can come up with something like the following:

II–V–I Eight-bar sequence in minor mode

TRACK 35

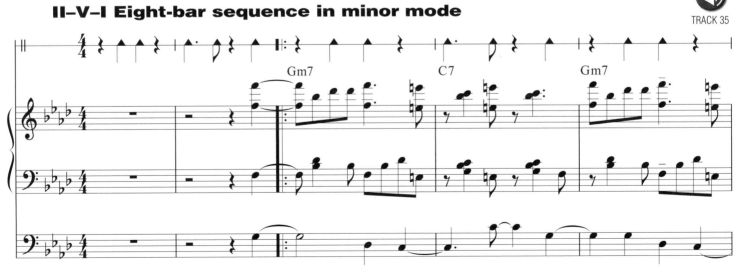

The following is a similar variation for the percussion solo section.

Percussion solo section sequence

TRACK 36

Of course, this can also be applied to a 3-2 clave environment. When the central part of the tune is in 3-2 clave (which is relatively rare, especially in New York City), a percussion solo in a similarly long montuno (this time in major mode) could be accompanied as in the next example:

Percussion solo section in 3-2 clave montuno

TRACK 37

* Some variations are present on repeat.

At this point let us recap and regroup the basic "guiding principles" described so far into five distinct categories:

1. Traditional tres figure
2. Chromatic descent
3. Seventh–third

4. Seventh–third plus parallel 10th
5. Fixed note repetition

TRACK 38   TRACK 39

A couple of extra examples should be analyzed before proceeding to the next chapter. The examples are on the audio only, and are thus a listening exercise. They offer us two further variations based on an eight-bar II–V–I sequence in major mode. A fair amount of improvisation and variation is displayed.

> *By now you should be able to listen to any example, analyze and recognize not only its clave structure, but also the guiding principle involved in the montuno section.*

Chapter 8

MONTUNOS FOR I–IV–V SEQUENCES: FO-FI

Besides the harmonic patterns studied in previous chapters, I–IV–V, both in minor and major keys, is another sequence very common in the salsa vocabulary.

When I first had the honor of playing with the Tito Puente Big Band, sitting in for a temporarily impaired Sonny Bravo, the first thing Tito told me was: "If you are a real salsa pianist, you have to know **fo-fi**…do you know **fo-fi** en Fa?" I answered: "W…what do you mean"? "Yes, fo-fi; don't you know it?" When I was about to give up in despair, everybody in the room burst into laughter. So Tito started singing: "fooo-fi-fo-fi-fo-fi-fo-fi-fi," onomatopoeically imitating the sound of a piano playing a I–IV–V figure in its most typical way, and fittingly asking me to play it in Fa, or F.

In Tito's practical joke, **fo** represents the octaves, and **fi** the less dominant chords.

Fo and fi

TRACK 40

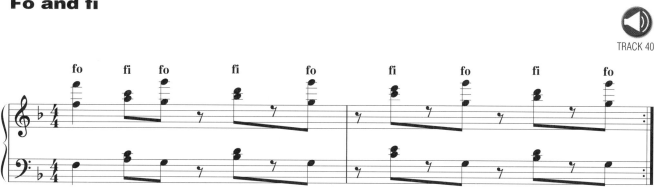

It is important to know that, just like in classical music and jazz, the IV chord can be replaced by its minor relative, II. Thus in F major, the IV chord (B♭) could be replaced by its relative minor, Gm.

Rhythmically, this pattern reminds us of the "Typical non-Latin figure" from Chapter 5 (p. 15). Again the question arises: Is this a 3-2 or a 2-3 clave montuno, and why? The answer is not simple!

Fo and fi with full band: 2-3 clave

TRACK 41

Some people might say that the bar where the first beat is played is the one with the "2" part of the clave, as in the previous example, the first bar.

On the other hand, one could argue that this could fit a 3-2 clave, given how the accents (octaves) of the first bar magically align with three hits of the rumba clave we are using in this next example.

Fo and fi with full band: 3-2 clave

TRACK 42

Let's see how the apparent contradiction of using such a pattern in 3-2 clave can be solved in an elegant way. Taking the music from the "Fo and fi with full band: 2-3 clave" example, we can keep playing, adding three more variations to the 3-2 version. In bars 3 and 4 we avoid playing on the first quarter note.

The next three examples feature two-bar patterns that would normally be played one after another to form one complete phrase. For the purpose of study, they have been broken up, with a separate count-off for each track, and each two-bar pattern is played twice.

Bars 3 and 4

TRACK 43

By shifting the first note to the "and" of beat one, we avoid playing on the first beat of the bar. In this case, it is logical to end the second part of the figure with an anticipated F octave (**X**), given the eighth-note rest at the beginning of the next bar. This anticipated F octave is in effect the beginning of the next pattern.

The following example represents a continuation from the previous example, in other words, bars 5 and 6, though you will hear a count off to make it easier to follow. In bar 6 we strongly establish a "2" segment of the clave by playing the first note of the bar (**X1**), then accenting the ④ and ⑤ hits of the clave (**X2** and **X3**):

Bars 5 and 6

Then again, starting in the last eighth note of bar 6, the pattern evolves into a more recognizable 3-2 clave figure. Track 46 plays bars 3–8 all together in one phrase, with no repeats.

Bars 7 and 8

Given instructions to play an F major I–IV–V in 2-3 clave, a knowledgeable pianist in a New York City band might instinctively play the following:

F major I-IV-V in 2-3 clave: New York City-style

This is safe and free of controversy, but rather simple and boring. In order to add some spice and energy, we could add a busier variation later on in the tune. This would most likely include arpeggiated harmonies, as in the following example:

Busier variation

TRACK 48

Note that in the second bar of this particular variation, a strong emphasis is made on the fourth beat (**X1**) which also happens to be the ⑤ hit of the 2-3 son clave. This is often referred to as **afinque**, something like "cementing" the 2-3 structure of the whole rhythm section. This effect is enhanced by keeping the first eighth of the third bar empty, thus giving the afinque a full dotted quarter note of duration. This is part of the vocabulary available to players and arrangers alike, but it is specifically oriented towards a son montuno type of arrangement, hence the emphasis on son clave (the ⑤ hit on beat 4). Some son montunos start precisely in this fashion: one or two instruments start ahead of the rest of the band, which then enters on the fourth beat. The fourth bar is played with the final octave, stressing the "and" of the fourth beat (**X2**), thus better distributing the time available in that bar and giving the whole pattern a stronger flow. These two versions can be played contiguously, thus creating in the process a four-bar pattern.

As in the sequence treated in the previous chapter (II–V–I), it is possible to obtain a percussive effect by emphasizing one note common to all chords involved. If it is a major I–IV–V, the most obvious choice would be the sixth of I.

Again, though not absolutely necessary, any two-bar pattern can become a four-bar pattern by slightly modifying the second sequence, including the addition of rhythmically intricate variations reminiscent of cowbell patterns.

Four-bar pattern in 2-3 clave

TRACK 49

Analyze very carefully bars 5–7 of this example. There are three similar motifs, each three beats in length, outlined in brackets above. Theoretically, you could use the second or third motif as the beginning of a new pattern, temporarily displacing the perceived downbeat of the piano figure, effectively having two downbeats. Some very expert pianists could use figures with three, five, seven, or any given number of eighths (other than of course eight) to displace the downbeat, achieving an amazing feeling of polyrhythmic acrobatics. These kinds of tricks, often used by Cuban pianists and other instrumentalists, have the unfortunate potential of creating enormous confusion, besides putting the pianist at the grave risk of being called disrespectful of clave. They should be attempted only if you are totally confident, and then at your own risk.

Towards the "peak" of the tune, the pianist can play ever-busier figures, in effect filling almost all the eighths of every bar.

In the very common situation where there is a percussion solo, pianists mostly resort to good old time-tested tres-style playing: very sparse unison figures that barely outline the chords, as seen in the next example:

Tres-style playing during a percussion solo

TRACK 50

We again see the afinque (**X**) on the fourth beat of bar 4. The very economic use of notes in this figure helps keep the band together, at the same time leaving space for the soloist to experiment.

Still, if the band needs more guidance and/or the tempo is too slow for such minimalist comping, the figure can become denser. A combination of arpeggios and chords might be the right dosage, using some elements seen in the second bar of the following example. One may also completely "spell out" the chords, leaving a few eighth notes untouched.

Arpeggio and chord combination

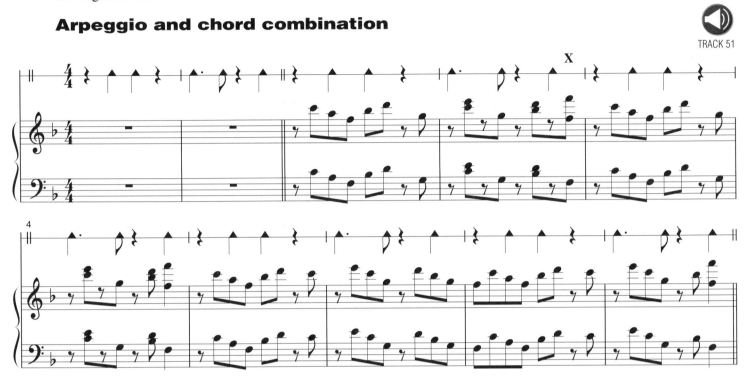

The next example is the same pattern as the "Four-bar pattern" (track 49), but in 3-2 clave.

Four-bar pattern in 3-2 clave

Minor Keys

Like most salsa patterns, track 51 can easily be translated into the minor mode, just making sure to play the major third of the V chord (in this case E♮ instead of E♭). Below is the minor version of track 51.

Arpeggio and chord combination: minor mode

TRACK 53

A good exercise would be to change the mode of all examples in this book. Let's try with the "Tres-style playing during a percussion solo" example (track 50):

Tres-style playing during a percussion solo: minor mode

TRACK 54

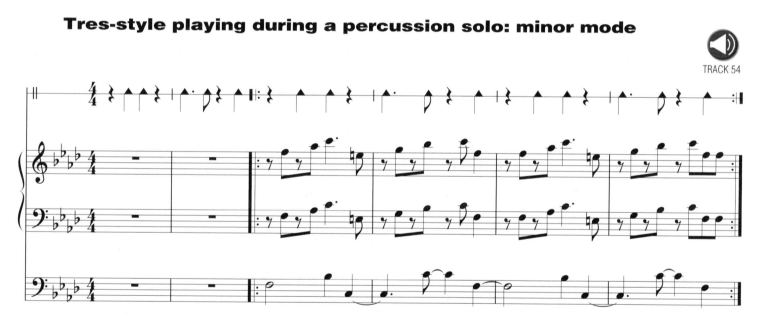

You will notice that in most of the examples in this book, changing them to minor will work just fine. Still, compared to the major mode, there are more diatonic changes that can be employed. For example, in F minor, the 7th of the tonic chord (E♭) can be major or minor, as in the V chord, the E is often changed to E♮ to make it dominant. The IV chord is also often turned into a major triad, thus, in F minor, the diatonic D♭ would be changed to D♮ producing a B♭ major triad.

Our next example shows only the first two bars of the piano part, but the audio plays a longer excerpt. This should suffice for our purpose. In the first bar of the piano part in the next example, the left hand plays a figure reminiscent of the single harmony descargas discussed earlier, playing a minor I. In this case, the seventh of this minor I chord moves down to the third of the major IV chord. The last bar of this example splices the V chord into a II–V sequence.

Single-harmony descargas in minor mode

As you can see, the right hand in this example often follows the movements of the left hand at the interval of a 10th. This harmonically more sophisticated pattern is a good example of the expanded possibilities in the minor mode. Note the ninth of the II chord at the end of bar 1: it is an A♮, which normally shouldn't belong in an F minor tonality. In the second bar, this A resolves to A♭ as part of a V chord full of alterations—A♭, which is the flat sixth; E♮, the major third, and D♭, the flat ninth. Also note that though there is an E♮ in the left hand, the right hand plays an E♭ on the "and" of 3, functioning as a "sharp ninth." Although such alterations are not unavailable in major tonalities, they sound more inherent to tunes in minor.

In Afro-Cuban music, this sophisticated harmonic treatment of otherwise very basic sequences is undoubtedly a result of its interaction with jazz, which has given rise to a new hybrid musical vocabulary. Musicians from both sides of the aisle have progressively engaged in this interaction from the very beginning of the twentieth century. Sometime in the middle of the century, a distinct new idiom affirmed its identity, first in the form baptized "Cubop" by the likes of Dizzy Gillespie, and later referred to as Latin jazz.

Chapter 9

PUTTING IT ALL TOGETHER

This chapter will summarize all the concepts learned so far with the help of a rather complex example: an eight-bar pattern with all possible combinations of II–V–I, and combined minor and major modes—in short, most of what we can expect in a professional salsa band. With this sequence, we can apply all the knowledge available literally at our fingertips.

Below is an example of the kind of information you are most likely going to get in a typical salsa chart.

Montuno (3-2 clave): chord progression

| | B♭m7 | | E♭7 | | A♭maj7 | | D♭maj7 | |
| | G⌀ | | C7 | | Fm7 | | C°7 | F7 | ‖ |

This could be either a part of the main body of the tune, or the central repetitive montuno section. This example features a series of sub-sequences, which in jazz would be immediately recognized, interpreted, and treated as individual II–V–Is. For example, the first three bars (B♭m7–E♭7–A♭maj7) can be understood as a II–V–I to A♭ instead of the IV–VII–III it appears to be in an F minor context. This type of harmonic sequence is ubiquitous in innumerable jazz standards, many of which have been, or could be, arranged for Latin jazz bands, in which case whatever knowledge of jazz you possess will come in handy. Conversely, the knowledge you gain from the Latin idiom can be easily applied to, or at least tested with, your jazz repertoire.

Now you are on your own in terms of what your figures are going to be. Let's first look at an easy version of the sequence. You will likely play one that heavily relies on the seventh of one chord resolving into the third of the next. You can go back to your knowledge of II–V–I in major and minor tonalities as seen in Chapter 6 to reaffirm this device. If the sequence appears in the head of the tune, it would very likely be in 3-2 clave.

> *By the way, 3-2 is the clave most commonly used for the main "body" of the tune: Introduction, head (with or without lyrics), interlude, second verse. Next, a break with an odd number of bars is played in order to invert the clave for the montuno section in 2-3. But this by no means rules out 3-2 montunos or 2-3 heads!*

Full Chart

TRACK 56

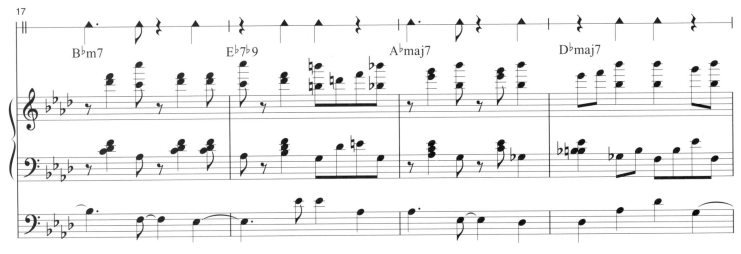

In the first eight bars (not including the two-measure clave count off), both hands follow a 7th–3rd–7th–3rd pattern. After that, the right hand opens up the harmony, playing a 10th plus octave above the left.

If this kind of sequence shows up in the more danceable montuno section towards the middle of the tune, there is a high likelihood that a 2-3 clave will be required from you. As has been stressed repeatedly, the most usual way to change from 2-3 to 3-2 is to add a break with an odd number of bars, sometimes up to nine. The obvious effect is that the second bar becomes the first. Again, if there are claves in the band actually playing the clave figure, the player doesn't even have to bother changing anything. He would keep playing his instrument, utterly oblivious to the turmoil happening around him. (Here it is important to say that a good rhythm section doesn't really need a clave player—the clave structure is *implied* in the way the other instrumentalists play their instruments, obeying the clave structure!) It is the harmonic rhythm that reinforces the new rhythmic structure of the tune. With the break including an odd number of bars, all of a sudden the clave has become 2-3, which will be especially welcomed by the dancers on the floor!

In the following example, every eight bars show a different variation of the same harmonic sequence in a 2-3 context. The excerpt includes all four examples, played continuously on the audio.

Four variations

In variation B, the same happens as in the second group of eight bars of the last "Full chart" example: the right hand opens up the harmony moving opposite of the left hand in the last bar of the first group. This gives us a parallel movement of a 10th plus an octave—in other words, seventh to third in the left, and ninth to fifth in the right.

Variation C goes back to the fixed-note principle, repeating one note in the right hand to give the pattern a more percussive character. In this case, the best candidate is E♭. Only in the sixth bar of this variation, when approaching the tonic via the dominant, does E♭ become E♮.

C

The last variation is very similar to B, but with a more interesting and audacious rhythmic interpretation.

Note that in the third bar of each variation, the A♭maj7 chord becomes an A♭ dominant 7 chord just before moving into D♭7. This makes it a brief II-V to a nonexistent
I that should be G♭ major. Instead of the imaginary G♭ chord, we have a Gm7♭5,
itself the legitimate II of the final II–V–I going home to F minor.

It is highly recommended that you practice these harmonic cycles in all twelve keys in order to conquer the
rhythmic as well as the harmonic challenges.

Chapter 10
SLOWING IT DOWN
GUAJIRA AND CHA-CHA,
SECOND-LEVEL SYNCOPATION

In this final chapter we will look into two distinct forms of Afro-Cuban dance rhythms that are closely related to the ones we have already discussed in depth, but have nonetheless a very specific language that is well worth understanding. The **cha-cha** and the **guajira** are two beautiful styles that are seldom used in recent fast-moving times.

The cha-cha originated in Havana, and it is associated with the danzón as well as its more danceable section, the mambo. Its dance step is one of the few in the Caribbean to include eighth notes, namely in the third quarter of the 4/4 bar, and not in the fourth quarter as it was taught in the U.S., where it became widely popular in the 1950s. Its name is said to imitate onomatopoetically the sound of a pair of scissors. Other people say it is the sound of the shoes rubbing the floor while dancing.

Although both the cha-cha and the guajira are relatively slow in tempo, the guajira tends to be the slower one, due to the sadness and gloominess it is meant to transmit. The dance attempts to paint this gloom by describing the hardships of everyday rural life endured by the peasants (also called "guajiros") of the mountainous region of eastern Cuba, the almost mythical Oriente. The guajira belongs to the family of rhythms associated with the son montuno. Some of its roots can be traced to Spain, more specifically to the Canary Islands, to which most of the Cuban population of European descent can trace its origins. It is arguably the blues of Latin music. Not surprisingly, it usually comes in minor keys, even as the most famous of all guajiras is in a major tonality: "Guantanamera." (The classification of this tune as a true guajira is not completely free of controversy. A Cuban teacher living in upstate New York decided, while teaching Spanish to young children, to put music to a poem written by Cuba's greatest poet, José Martí, to make it easier for them to learn. Later, North American singer-songwriter Pete Seeger, heard the result, made some refinements, and added it to his repertoire.)

Sometimes guajira and cha-cha are hard to tell apart. The pulse of the guajira tends to be more of a 2/2, alla breve, while the cha-cha no doubt follows a 4/4 pulse. Another important difference is the instrumentation. Small combos—consisting of tres, guitar, bongos, and a set of maracas—usually play rural guajiras. The cha-cha evolved in an urban environment distinguished by a strong African influence and easy access to European instruments like strings, woodwinds, brass, and—relevant for us—piano.

The slow tempo of both styles makes for a good exercise, not only of the material already used, but also in the use of hemiolas and double-time figures that an expert pianist can later apply to medium- and fast-tempo salsa.

For didactic purposes, our cha-cha will be in 2-3 clave and the guajira in 3-2. This way we will have the possibility to practice both claves at slow tempos.

Guajira

Though most guajiras are played in 2-3, some of them come in 3-2. More than anywhere, the concept of the bar where the first beat is played automatically becoming the "2" part of the clave is once again put into question. The following is one example:

Guajira in 3-2 clave

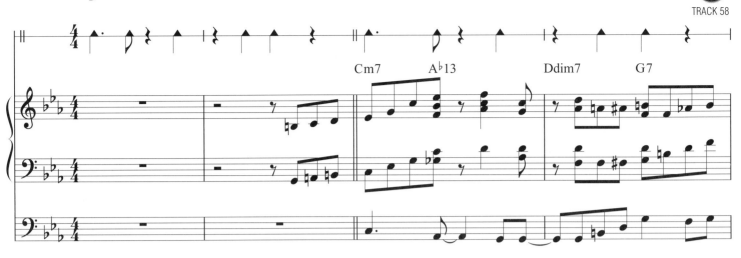

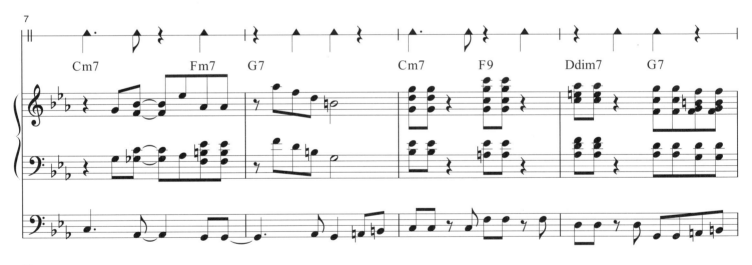

48

At this slow tempo the figures are busier—as in bar 2, which has only one open eighth note. The G7 in bar 8 is reinforced with a long half-note duration, preparing the band for a good percussion solo with heavy chords on beats 1 and 3 of bar 9 (the Cm7) for two bars, and then two bars of regular montuno. In bars 11 and 15, we see small groups of sixteenth notes, at two different stages of the bar. As you can see, both times this happens when a quarter or a dotted quarter note would otherwise counter the momentum of the piece in an anticlimactic way. These kinds of tricks are often used by expert Cuban pianists to add yet another level to the sense of syncopation. It is sometimes used, to great effect, in faster tempos. Try it out first in the styles discussed in this chapter, and only later start applying it to other rhythms!

Cha-cha

Next, we will analyze two different versions of the same short piece: first, a rather simple, academic offering of a typical cha-cha, and then a more sophisticated and complex variation.

Simple cha-cha

TRACK 59

The first eight bars show an extended II-V-I in major mode, showcasing an archetypical figure that echoes the sound and rhythmic characteristics of the small cha-cha bell played by the timbales player. In this very percussive pattern, the two hands never play simultaneously—the player alternates left and right, like in a drummer's paradiddle exercise, with the right hand playing mostly on beats 1 and 3, while the left plays on the upbeats of all four quarter notes.

In order to better visualize and understand this interesting pattern, it might help to write the two-bar piano part in a single system:

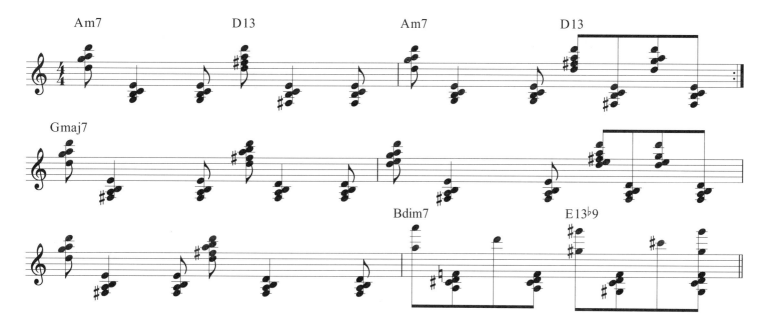

In bar 8 of "Simple cha-cha," the piano prepares a change not only to the minor mode, but also to a more conventional way of playing, in essence turning the piece into something of a fast guajira. The general rules studied in preceding chapters apply here too. In this slower tempo, you will be able to review your understanding of 2-3 clave, like looking at it under a magnifying glass. Bars 9–11 seem pretty straightforward, applying the principle of playing the first beat of "2" bar of 2-3. In bar 12 the octaves on the last two eighth notes of the bar anticipate the downbeat of bar 13, leaving both measures 13 and 14 without a downbeat note. The "2" part of the clave in bar 13 is then appropriately reinforced with the descending octave movement leading to the third beat.

Measures 11–14 of "simple cha-cha"

Once you have understood and mastered the basic structures of these patterns, you can relish the possibilities that the slow tempo of this style has to offer, in terms of what may be referred to as "second level syncopation." The pianist should be able to create variations of the basic pattern without changing its original underlying character.

Complex cha-cha variation

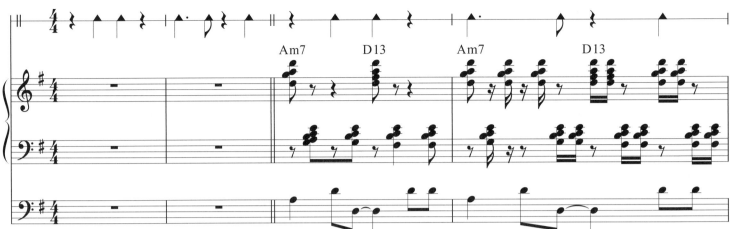

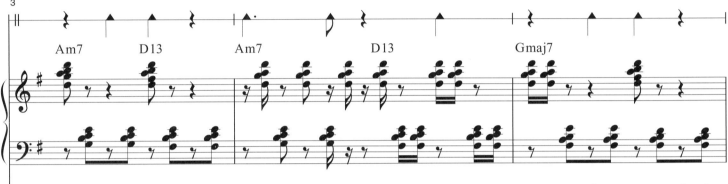

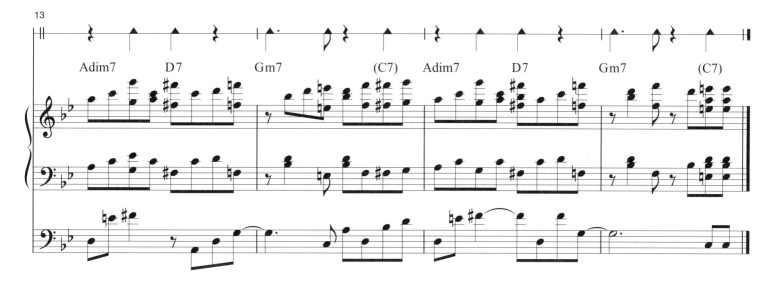

Again, the pattern in the first half is easier to visualize as in the following:

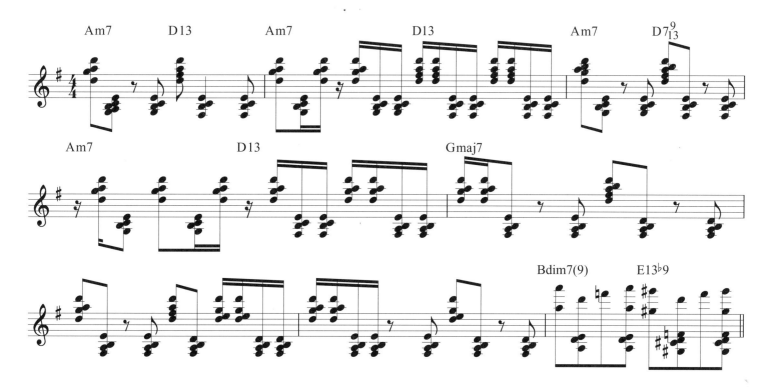

Bar 11 features a very difficult—some would say idiosyncratic—variation, with a quarter-note-triplet starting on an eighth-note upbeat and ending on the last eighth of the bar. Displaced triplets and other tuplets sound very interesting and are used during solos, but also in performance, composition, and arrangements in a Latin jazz context. Use at your own risk in a salsa band!

All these rhythmic variations add a very interesting touch to the section. Of course, this example gives you as many variations as possible in a few bars. In a strictly salsa environment, this kind of playing could prove distracting to singers and dancers if overused. It is recommended to use it sparingly behind vocals and more intensely, for example, during instrumental solos. Moreover, the ideas here are often used by composers and arrangers alike to take the music away from the stereotypical and formulaic.

EPILOGUE

I must confess that although from early on I've strived to learn as much as possible from the piano greats of times past and present, I also learned a significant portion of the knowledge conveyed in this book from accomplished drummers and percussionists. They are the masters of rhythmic experimentation. That's not to say that I haven't heard unbelievable rhythmic acrobatics from the hands of great pianists! As I mentioned at the beginning of this book, in Afro-Cuban music, the piano is just as much a percussion instrument as it is a melodic and harmonic one. This book should have helped you not only to learn the basics, but also, once that first stage is mastered, to get away from the obvious. Hopefully this was achieved without disrespecting traditions received from the many famous and anonymous creators of this style, those who probably wouldn't mind us taking it another step forward. While writing this book, as I approached the "light at the end of the tunnel," I could not help but notice that I was learning just as much as I was hoping to teach. Trying to describe a situation, a pattern, or any detail relevant to the art of the Latin piano involved a search for words, concepts, history, and often led to the discovery of contradicting opinions on the matter. I have come to understand two things:

1. In popular culture "knowledge" is, more than in other fields, a very subjective matter.

2. More important than anything: teaching is learning.

Hey, pass it on!

KEYBOARD STYLE SERIES

THE COMPLETE GUIDE!

These book/audio packs provide focused lessons that contain valuable how-to insight, essential playing tips, and beneficial information for all players. From comping to soloing, comprehensive treatment is given to each subject. The companion audio features many of the examples in the book performed either solo or with a full band.

BEBOP JAZZ PIANO
by John Valerio

This book provides detailed information for bebop and jazz keyboardists on: chords and voicings, harmony and chord progressions, scales and tonality, common melodic figures and patterns, comping, characteristic tunes, the styles of Bud Powell and Thelonious Monk, and more.

00290535 Book/Online Audio $21.99

BEGINNING ROCK KEYBOARD
by Mark Harrison

This comprehensive book/audio package will teach you the basic skills needed to play beginning rock keyboard. From comping to soloing, you'll learn the theory, the tools, and the techniques used by the pros. The accompanying audio demonstrates most of the music examples in the book.

00311922 Book/Online Audio $16.99

BLUES PIANO
by Mark Harrison

With this book/audio pack, you'll learn the theory, the tools, and even the tricks that the pros use to play the blues. Covers: scales and chords; left-hand patterns; walking bass; endings and turnarounds; right-hand techniques; how to solo with blues scales; crossover licks; and more.

00311007 Book/Online Audio $22.99

BOOGIE-WOOGIE PIANO
by Todd Lowry

From learning the basic chord progressions to inventing your own melodic riffs, you'll learn the theory, tools and techniques used by the genre's best practicioners.

00117067 Book/Online Audio $17.99

BRAZILIAN PIANO
by Robert Willey and Alfredo Cardim

Brazilian Piano teaches elements of some of the most appealing Brazilian musical styles: choro, samba, and bossa nova. It starts with rhythmic training to develop the fundamental groove of Brazilian music.

00311469 Book/Online Audio $19.99

CONTEMPORARY JAZZ PIANO
by Mark Harrison

From comping to soloing, you'll learn the theory, the tools, and the techniques used by the pros. The full band tracks on the audio feature the rhythm section on the left channel and the piano on the right channel, so that you can play along with the band.

00311848 Book/Online Audio $19.99

COUNTRY PIANO
by Mark Harrison

Learn the theory, the tools, and the tricks used by the pros to get that authentic country sound. This book/audio pack covers: scales and chords, walkup and walkdown patterns, comping in traditional and modern country, Nashville "fretted piano" techniques and more.

00311052 Book/Online Audio $19.99

GOSPEL PIANO
by Kurt Cowling

Discover the tools you need to play in a variety of authentic gospel styles, through a study of rhythmic devices, grooves, melodic and harmonic techniques, and formal design. The accompanying audio features over 90 tracks, including piano examples as well as the full gospel band.

00311327 Book/Online Adio $19.99

INTRO TO JAZZ PIANO
by Mark Harrison

From comping to soloing, you'll learn the theory, the tools, and the techniques used by the pros. The accompanying audio demonstrates most of the music examples in the book. The full band tracks feature the rhythm section on the left channel and the piano on the right channel, so that you can play along with the band.

00312088 Book/Online Audio $19.99

JAZZ-BLUES PIANO
by Mark Harrison

This comprehensive book will teach you the basic skills needed to play jazz-blues piano. Topics covered include: scales and chords • harmony and voicings • progressions and comping • melodies and soloing • characteristic stylings.

00311243 Book/Online Audio $19.99

JAZZ-ROCK KEYBOARD
by T. Lavitz

Learn what goes into mixing the power and drive of rock music with the artistic elements of jazz improvisation in this comprehensive book and CD package. This instructional tool delves into scales and modes, and how they can be used with various chord progressions to develop the best in soloing chops.

00290536 Book/CD Pack..........................$17.95

LATIN JAZZ PIANO
by John Valerio

This book is divided into three sections. The first covers Afro-Cuban (Afro-Caribbean) jazz, the second section deals with Brazilian influenced jazz – Bossa Nova and Samba, and the third contains lead sheets of the tunes and instructions for the play-along audio.

00311345 Book/Online Audio $19.99

MODERN POP KEYBOARD
by Mark Harrison

From chordal comping to arpeggios and ostinatos, from grand piano to synth pads, you'll learn the theory, the tools, and the techniques used by the pros. The online audio demonstrates most of the music examples in the book.

00146596 Book/Online Audio $19.99

NEW AGE PIANO
by Todd Lowry

From melodic development to chord progressions to left-hand accompaniment patterns, you'll learn the theory, the tools and the techniques used by the pros. The accompanying 96-track CD demonstrates most of the music examples in the book.

00117322 Book/CD Pack..........................$16.99

HAL•LEONARD®

Prices, contents, and availability subject to change without notice.

www.halleonard.com

POST-BOP JAZZ PIANO
by John Valerio

This book/audio pack will teach you the basic skills needed to play post-bop jazz piano. Learn the theory, the tools, and the tricks used by the pros to play in the style of Bill Evans, Thelonious Monk, Herbie Hancock, McCoy Tyner, Chick Corea and others. Topics covered include: chord voicings, scales and tonality, modality, and more.

00311005 Book/Online Audio $19.99

PROGRESSIVE ROCK KEYBOARD
by Dan Maske

You'll learn how soloing techniques, form, rhythmic and metrical devices, harmony, and counterpoint all come together to make this style of rock the unique and exciting genre it is.

00311307 Book/Online Audio $19.99

R&B KEYBOARD
by Mark Harrison

From soul to funk to disco to pop, you'll learn the theory, the tools, and the tricks used by the pros with this book/audio pack. Topics covered include: scales and chords, harmony and voicings, progressions and comping, rhythmic concepts, characteristic stylings, the development of R&B, and more! Includes seven songs.

00310881 Book/Online Audio $22.99

ROCK KEYBOARD
by Scott Miller

Learn to comp or solo in any of your favorite rock styles. Listen to the audio to hear your parts fit in with the total groove of the band. Includes 99 tracks! Covers: classic rock, pop/rock, blues rock, Southern rock, hard rock, progressive rock, alternative rock and heavy metal.

00310823 Book/Online Audio $17.99

ROCK 'N' ROLL PIANO
by Andy Vinter

Take your place alongside Fats Domino, Jerry Lee Lewis, Little Richard, and other legendary players of the '50s and '60s! This book/audio pack covers: left-hand patterns; basic rock 'n' roll progressions; right-hand techniques; straight eighths vs. swing eighths; glisses, crushed notes, rolls, note clusters and more. Includes six complete tunes.

00310912 Book/Online Audio $19.99

SALSA PIANO
by Hector Martignon

From traditional Cuban music to the more modern Puerto Rican and New York styles, you'll learn the all-important rhythmic patterns of salsa and how to apply them to the piano. The book provides historical, geographical and cultural background info, and the 50+-tracks includes piano examples and a full salsa band percussion section.

00311049 Book/Online Audio $19.99

SMOOTH JAZZ PIANO
by Mark Harrison

Learn the skills you need to play smooth jazz piano – the theory, the tools, and the tricks used by the pros. Topics covered include: scales and chords; harmony and voicings; progressions and comping; rhythmic concepts; melodies and soloing; characteristic stylings; discussions on jazz evolution.

00311095 Book/Online Audio $19.99

STRIDE & SWING PIANO
by John Valerio

Learn the styles of the stride and swing piano masters, such as Scott Joplin, Jimmy Yancey, Pete Johnson, Jelly Roll Morton, James P. Johnson, Fats Waller, Teddy Wilson, and Art Tatum. This book/audio pack covers classic ragtime, early blues and boogie woogie, New Orleans jazz and more. Includes 14 songs.

00310882 Book/Online Audio $22.99

WORSHIP PIANO
by Bob Kauflin

From chord inversions to color tones, from rhythmic patterns to the Nashville Numbering System, you'll learn the tools and techniques needed to play piano or keyboard in a modern worship setting.

00311425 Book/Online Audio $19.99